Football's Finest

Bob Italia

Published by Abdo & Daughters, 4940 Viking Dr., Suite 622, Minnesota 55435.

Library bound edition distributed by Rockbottom Books, Pentagon Tower, P.O. Box 36036, Minneapolis, Minnesota 55435.

Printed in the United States.

Cover Photo: Allsport
Inside Photos: Allsport 5, 6, 8, 11, 13, 14, 15, 16, 17, 18, 19, 21, 22, 27, 28, 31, 32, 33, 34.
   SportsChrome 24, 26, 34.
   NFL Photos 9, 23, 25, 29.

Edited by Rosemary Wallner

Italia, Robert, 1955-
   Football's Finest / written by Bob Italia.
      p.   cm -- (The Year in sports)
   Includes bibliographical references and index.
   ISBN 1-56239-242-5
   1. Football players--United States--Biography--Juvenile literature. 2. Football--United States--History--Juvenile literature. I. Title. II. Series: Year in sports (Edina, Minn.)
   GV939.A1I83   1993
   796.332' 092' 2--dc20   93-2285
   [B]   CIP
                                                        AC

Contents

PhyC Love
Kim

Football Field Diagram

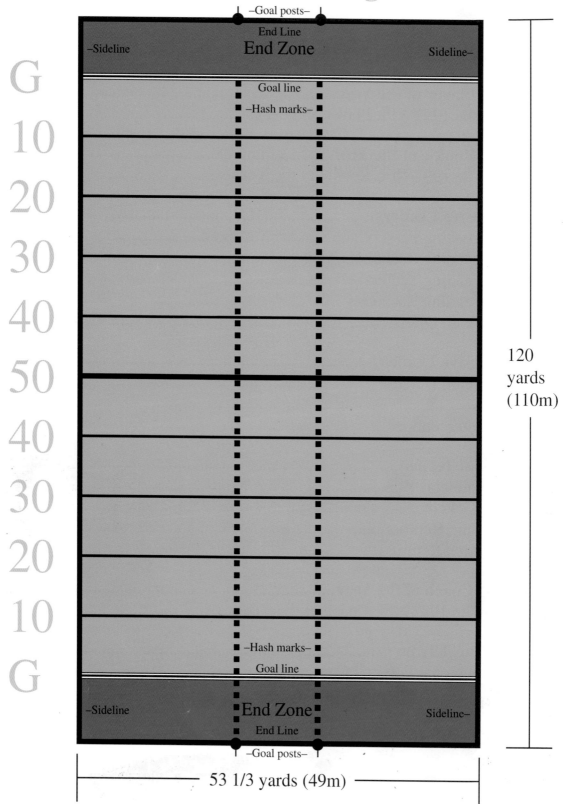

How NFL Awards
Are Determined

In any sport, players strive to do their best each season. After the season ends, sportswriters, league players, and coaches look at statistics and compare performances. That's when the fans find out who was the best of the best.

The National Football League (NFL) does not officially recognize any postseason awards for players or coaches. But sportswriters and organizations such as the Associated Press (AP) and United Press International (UPI) recognize player and coach excellence. Other organizations that give out awards are *The Sporting News* magazine, and the Pro Football Writers of America (PFWA). NFL Player of the Year awards are presented by the Maxwell Club of Philadelphia (the Bert Bell Award) and the NFL Players Association (Jim Thorpe Trophy).

NFL Player of the Year

The Player of the Year Award honors one player who has contributed the most to his team's success. Quarterbacks who throw many touchdown passes or running backs who win the rushing title are usually the winners of this honor.

Walter Payton was the 1977 NFL Player of the Year.

A list of past winners attests to this fact: running backs Thurman Thomas and Barry Sanders (1991), quarterbacks Randall Cunningham and Joe Montana (1990), quarterback Dan Marino (1984), running back Earl Campbell (1979), and running back Walter Payton (1977).

Occasionally, a dominant defensive player will win the award: linebacker Lawrence Taylor (1986), tackle Merlin Olsen (1974), and tackle Alan Page (1971). But defensive players don't score many touchdowns or throw game-winning passes, and that usually influences the voting.

Since 1938, quarterbacks have been named Player of the Year on 39 occasions, running backs 23 times. Multiple winners include running back Jim Brown (4), quarterbacks Johnny Unitas and Y.A. Tittle (3), running backs Earl Campbell (2) and Walter Payton (2), quarterbacks Randall Cunningham (2), Joe Montana (2), Joe Theisman (2), Otto Graham (2), and end Don Hutson (2).

The first Player of the Year award was presented in 1938 to center Mel Hein of the New York Giants. That year, the award was called the Joe F. Carr Trophy (Carr was the NFL president from 1921-1939).

The Carr Trophy lasted thru 1946. From 1947 to 1952, no award was given. Then in 1953, UPI took over the voting. In 1957, AP gave its own award to Jim Brown while UPI voted for Y.A.Tittle. In 1959, the Maxwell Club added to the confusion by awarding their Bert Bell Trophy to Johnny Unitas. (UPI also selected Unitas while AP chose quarterback Charley Conerly.)

UPI gave their last NFL Player of the Year award in 1969 to quarterback Roman Gabriel. Since 1970, UPI has given two separate Player of the Year awards, one to the National Football Conference (NFC) and one to the American Football Conference (AFC).

In 1976, the PFWA joined the NFL Player of the Year voting when it selected quarterback Bert Jones. Whether you agree with AP, UPI, the Maxwell Club, or the PFWA, you can be sure that the winner is one of football's finest players.

The 1992 NFL Player of the Year

There was no debate in 1992 among the voters. The NFL Player of the Year award went to San Francisco 49er quarterback Steve Young.

Young made it easy for the voters. He threw 384 passes and completed 256 of them (66.7 percent). Twenty-five of his passes were for touchdowns (tops in the NFL). Young led his team to the NFC Championship game where they lost a close contest to the Dallas Cowboys. Even more impressive, Young threw only 7 interceptions all year. Only Atlanta Falcon quarterback Chris Miller had thrown less (6).

NFL Player of the Year	
Year	**Pos.**
1992 Steve Young	QB
1991 Thurman Thomas	RB
Barry Sanders	RB
1990 Randall Cunningham	QB
Joe Montana	QB
1989 Joe Montana	QB
1988 Boomer Esiason	QB
Randall Cunningham	QB

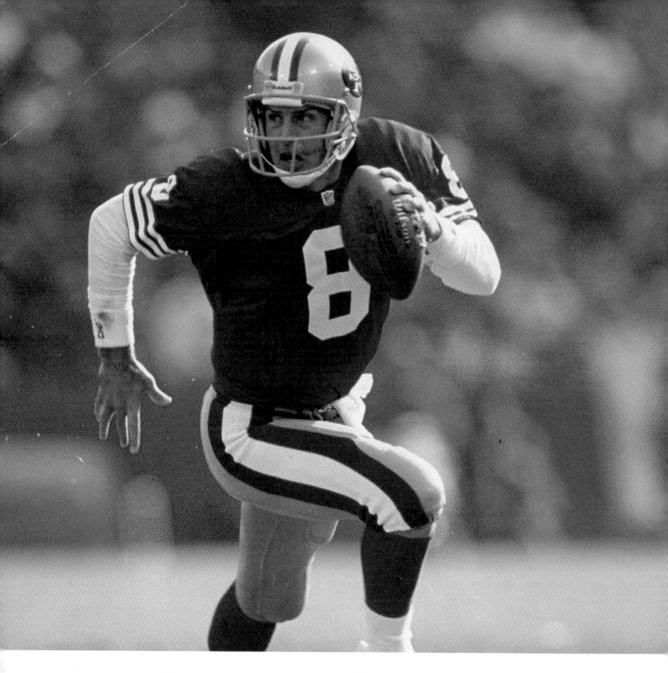

Steve Young – the 1992 NFL Player of the Year.

Remarkably, Steve Young won the award playing in the shadow of two-time Player of the Year Joe Montana. Montana, out for the year with an injured right elbow, is perhaps the NFL's greatest quarterback. Young could have easily folded under such pressure. Instead, he had his best season ever.

NFL Rookie of the Year

The NFL Rookie of the Year award honors the most promising and productive first-year talent. Rookies usually arrive in the NFL from the college draft. They are not always expected to contribute to their team's success. Sometimes it takes years before a player blossoms into a strong and intelligent football player. Other times, however, rookies excel on the field. They become star players themselves. Often they show veteran players a thing or two about the game of football.

Many outstanding rookies become outstanding veteran players. Barry Sanders (1989), Jerry Rice (1985), Earl Campbell (1978), and Mike Ditka (1961) were all winning rookies. They became some of the greatest players of all time.

Superstar Emmitt Smith was not a Rookie of the Year.

Winning Rookie of the Year honors does not guarantee a successful career, however. What ever happened to rookie winners Earl Faison (1961), Mike Thomas (1975), or George Rogers (1981)?

And just because a player isn't named Rookie of the Year does not mean he will be unsuccessful. Joe Montana, Dan Marino, and Walter Payton (just to name a few) did not receive the award. Yet they became well known and respected players.

UPI created the NFL Rookie of the Year award in 1955. They presented the first award to Alan Ameche of the Baltimore Colts.

Today *The Sporting News* NFL Rookie of the Year award is recognized as a top honor because NFL player votes determine the winner.

The 1992 NFL Rookie of the Year

The 1992 *Sporting News* NFL Rookie of the Year was defensive tackle Santana Dotson of the Tampa Bay Buccaneers. Dotson was a fifth-round draft pick. But in Tampa's first game, Dotson made a big impression on the rest of the league. He sacked Phoenix Cardinal quarterback Timm Rosenbach—and knocked him out for the season.

The 6-foot 4-inch, 270-pound Dotson went on to lead his team in sacks (10)—a Tampa Bay rookie record. He also led the Bucs in tackles for losses (11) and quarterback pressures (25). Dotson also recovered two fumbles, one of which he returned for a touchdown.

A dramatic moment for Dotson came in Week 4 of the 1992 season. The Detroit Lions led the Bucs 16-13 midway through the fourth quarter and controlled the ball. Detroit quarterback Rodney Peete tried to handoff to running back Barry Sanders, but the ball bounced off Sanders' hip. Dotson recovered the botched handoff. He burst through a crowd of players and lumbered 42 yards for the score. Tampa Bay went on to a shocking 27-23 win.

"I knew the talent I had," Dotson said. "The main thing I was hoping for was the opportunity and I got that in Tampa. I feel real good about the things I did my rookie season. The main thing is to get out and work that much harder next season. I don't want to be part of the ill-fated sophomore jinx."

Santana Dotson — the 1992 NFL Rookie of the Year.

Offensive Leaders

A touchdown is one of the most exciting events in football. It usually comes dramatically, often unexpectedly—and can instantly turn a loss into a win.

Players who score touchdowns are often the most popular players in football. They are usually running backs or wide receivers. Running backs who rack up rushing yardage and touchdowns increase their chances for the Player of the Year award. The best running backs can control the ball—and the game—with their relentless running. Some running backs, like Kansas City's Christian Okoye, like to punish defensive players with their bruising, pounding, rushing style. Other running backs, like Detroit's Barry Sanders, combine a power rush with shifty, slashing moves and pure bursts of speed.

Wide receivers have less of a chance to win Player of the Year honors because they don't handle the ball as often as running backs or quarterbacks. But occasionally, a wide receiver can dominate the game, like Jerry Rice did in 1987.

Equally popular with football fans are the quarterbacks. They are the field generals, the team leaders. Their decisions to throw or run the ball determine the fate of the game. If a quarterback throws for many touchdown passes or yardage and plays for a winning team, he has a good chance of winning the Player of the Year award. The 1992 winner, Steve Young, is a good example.

NFL Leading Passers							
Player	Att.	Comp.	Pct.	Yds.	TD.	Int.	Pts.
Steve Young, San Francisco 49ers	402	268	66.7	3,465	25	7	107.0
Chris Miller, Atlanta Falcons	253	152	60.1	1,739	15	6	90.7
Troy Aikman, Dallas Cowboys	473	302	63.8	3,445	23	14	89.5
Warren Moon, Houston Oilers	346	224	64.7	2,521	18	12	89.3
Randall Cunningham, Philadelphia Eagles	384	233	60.7	2,775	19	11	87.3

Leading Passers

In 1992, no one passed the football better than NFC player Steve Young. Young, of the San Francisco 49ers, recorded one of the best statistical seasons for a quarterback in NFL history. He led the league in touchdown passes (25), completion percentage (66.7), average gain per pass play (8.62 yards), and interception percentage (1.7, or 7 in 402 attempts). He also ran for 537 yards and led the NFL by averaging 7.1 yards per carry.

In the AFC, Houston Oiler Warren Moon finished as the conference's top passer. He completed 224 of 346 passes for 2,521 total yards and a 64.7 completion percentage. Eighteen of his passes went for touchdowns, while 12 were intercepted.

In 1992, Warren Moon led the AFC in passing.

Leading Rushers

Barry Foster led the AFC in rushing.

It was a close race in 1992. But Emmitt Smith of the Dallas Cowboys won his second consecutive NFL rushing title. Smith and Pittsburgh's Barry Foster each had a chance to win the title on the last day. Smith came up with the big game, rushing for 131 yards against the Chicago Bears.

For the season, Smith racked up 1,713 yards on 373 attempts for a 4.6 yard average. He also scored a whopping 18 touchdowns—one of which came on a 68-yard romp.

Barry Foster was the leading AFC rusher. He finished with 1,690 yards on 390 attempts for a 4.3 yard average. He scored 11 touchdowns and had a 69-yard TD run.

NFL Leading Rushers

Player	Att.	Yds.	Avg.	Long	TD.
Emmitt Smith, Dallas Cowboys	373	1,713	4.6	68	18
Barry Foster, Pittsburgh Steelers	390	1,690	4.3	69	11
Thurman Thomas, Buffalo Bills	312	1,487	4.8	44	9
Barry Sanders, Detroit Lions	312	1,352	4.3	55	9
Lorenzo White, Houston Oilers	265	1,226	4.6	44	7

Emmitt Smith — the 1992 NFL rushing leader.

Leading Scorers

When it came to scoring touchdowns in 1992, no one came close to Emmitt Smith. His 19 total touchdowns (18 rushing, 1 pass reception) and 114 total points were by far the best in the NFL. The NFC's Terry Allen of the Minnesota Vikings was a distant second with 90 points, followed by Rodney Hampton of the New York Giants (84 points) and Sterling Sharpe of the Green Bay Packers (78 points).

Buffalo Bills' Thurman Thomas won the AFC's scoring race with 72 points. The versatile Thomas rushed for 9 TD's and scored 3 more with his pass-catching ability. Barry Foster finished second with 11 rushing touchdowns for 66 points.

Emmitt Smith (left) and Terry Allen (right) were the NFL's leading scorers.

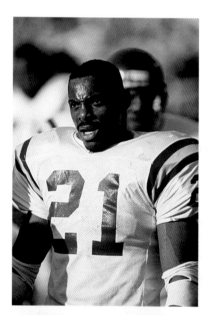

NFL Leading Scorers

Player	TD	Rush	Rec.	Pts.
Emmitt Smith, Dallas Cowboys	19	18	1	114
Terry Allen, Minnesota Vikings	15	13	2	90
Rodney Hampton, New York Giants	14	14	0	84
Sterling Sharpe, Green Bay Packers	13	0	13	78
Thurman Thomas, Buffalo Bills	12	9	3	72

Leading Receivers

In 1992, the NFC's Sterling Sharpe of the Green Bay Packers had a sterling season catching the ball. This tall, speedy wide receiver caught a league-record 108 passes for 1,461 yards and a 13.5 yard average. (Washington Redskin receiver Art Monk had held the record with 106 catches in one season.) Sharpe's 13 touchdowns were also tops for receivers. His longest reception came on a 76-yard scoring romp. The NFC's Andre Rison of the Atlanta Falcons finished second in the NFL with 93 catches for 1,121 total yards and 11 touchdowns.

No one caught more passes in 1992 than Sterling Sharpe.

In the AFC, Haywood Jeffires of the Houston Oilers snatched a conference-best 90 passes for 913 yards and a 10.1 yard average. His longest reception went for 47 yards, and he racked up 9 touchdowns. Teammate Curtis Duncan was second with 82 receptions for 954 yards and an 11.6 yard average.

NFL Leading Receivers

Player	No.	Yds.	Avg.	Long	TD
Sterling Sharpe, Green Bay Packers	108	1,461	13.5	76	13
Andre Rison, Atlanta Falcons	93	1,121	12.1	71	11
Haywood Jeffires, Houston Oilers	90	913	10.1	47	9
Jerry Rice, San Francisco 49ers	84	1,201	14.3	80	10
Curtis Duncan, Houston Oilers	82	954	11.6	72	1

In 1992, the Buffalo Bills had the AFC's best offense.

Team Offense

The San Francisco 49ers had the top-rated offense in the NFC and the NFL in 1992. Led by NFL Player of the Year Steve Young and wide receiver Jerry Rice, the 49ers racked up 6,195 total yards—2,315 rushing yards (3rd) and 3,880 passing yards (3rd). They were the top passing team in the NFC and second-best in rushing. Ricky Watters led the team in rushing with 1,013 yards on 206 carries and 9 touchdowns. Rice finished with 84 catches for 1,201 yards and 10 touchdowns.

In the AFC, the Buffalo Bills had the best overall offense (5,893) and second-best in the NFL. Players such as quarterback Jim Kelly, running back Thurman Thomas, and wide receiver Andre Reed helped Buffalo finish first in the NFL in total rushing yards (2,436) and third in the conference in passing yards (3,457).

NFL Team Offense			
Team	**Total**	**Rush**	**Pass**
San Francisco 49ers	6,195	2,315	3,880
Buffalo Bills	5,893	2,436	3,457
Houston Oilers	5,655	1,626	4,025
Dallas Cowboys	5,606	2,121	3,485
Miami Dolphins	5,500	1,525	3,975

The San Francisco 49ers had the NFL's best offense.

Defensive Leaders

Defense is just as important in football as it is in other sports. Yet defense rarely gets the same attention as a game-winning touchdown pass or a runner's game-by-game statistics. In football, the offense gets most of the glory.

But without solid and sparkling defensive plays, no football team can hope to win a championship. The strongest teams are the ones with rock-solid defensive lines that can stop the greatest running backs and harass the deadliest quarterbacks. They have hard-hitting linebackers who can plug the holes in the defensive line, and swift defensive backs who can go step-for-step with the fleetest wide receivers.

The best defenders usually lead their conferences in sacks, fumble recoveries, tackles, or interceptions. Their outstanding play in the field places them head and shoulders above their peers, and adds to their overall value to the team.

Team Defense

Not surprisingly, the 1992 Super Bowl champion Dallas Cowboys had the best defense in the NFC and the NFL. Players such as defensive tackle Russell Maryland, linebacker Ken Norton, and safety Thomas Everett anchored a team that gave up an average of only 77.8 rushing yards per game—tops in the NFL. Only three teams—Philadelphia, Detroit, and the Los Angeles Rams—gained more than 100 rushing yards against the Cowboy defense during the regular season. Dallas also finished fifth in passing yards allowed with a 168.1 yards-per-game average.

The Cowboys had the NFL's toughest defense in 1992.

In the AFC, the Houston Oilers had the best overall defense. Players such as cornerback Chris Dishman, linebacker Al Smith, and tackle Ray Childress helped Houston finish second in the conference in total passing yards allowed (2,577) and fifth in rushing yards allowed (1,634).

NFL Team Defense

Team	Total	Rush	Pass
Dallas Cowboys	3,933	1,244	2,689
New Orleans Saints	4,075	1,605	2,470
Houston Oilers	4,211	1,634	2,577
San Diego Chargers	4,227	1,395	2,832
Kansas City Chiefs	4,324	1,787	2,537

Sacks

To be a sack leader, players must not only be big and powerful, they must also be quick. Offensive lines often double-team defensive players who have a talent for rushing the quarterback. To defeat this tactic, sack leaders develop lightning-fast moves. But when all else fails, these players will use their brute strength to push their way into the opponent's backfield.

No one terrorized quarterbacks in 1992 more than Philadelphia Eagle defensive end Clyde Simmons. The 6-foot, 6-inch, 280-pound Simmons led the NFL and the NFC with 19 sacks. Tim Harris of the San Francisco 49ers finished second inthe NFC with 17 sacks.

Defensive end Leslie O'Neal of the San Diego Chargers led the AFC with 17 sacks. Denver linebacker Simon Fletcher finished second in the conference with 16 sacks.

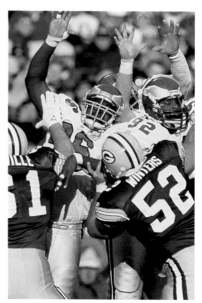

Clyde Simmons (center) was the NFL's most fearsome pass rusher.

NFL Sack Leaders	
Player	**Sacks**
Clyde Simmons, Philadelphia Eagles	19.0
Tim Harris, San Francisco 49ers	17.0
Leslie O'Neal, San Diego Chargers	17.0
Simon Fletcher, Denver Broncos	16.0
William Martin, New Orleans Saints	15.5

NFL Interception Leaders

Player	Int.	Yds.	Long	TD
Audray McMillian, Minnesota Vikings	8	157	51	2
Henry Jones, Buffalo Bills	8	263	82	2
Donnell Woolford, Chicago Bears	7	67	32	0
Eugene Robinson, Seattle Seahawks	7	126	49	0
Dale Carter, Kansas City Chiefs	7	65	36	1

Interceptions

Top pass defenders stick to offensive receivers like glue. Even more, they must anticipate where the football will be thrown and step in front of a receiver without interfering on the play. Their dramatic plays halt opponent's scoring drives—and sometimes end up as touchdowns.

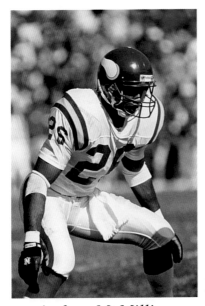

Audray McMillian intercepted 8 passes in 1992.

In 1992, cornerback Audray McMillian of the NFC's Minnesota Vikings swiped 8 passes, which tied for first in the NFL. McMillian's longest interception return was 51 yards—good for a touchdown. In all, McMillian scored two touchdowns and returned interceptions for 157 yards.

In the AFC, safety Henry Jones of the Buffalo Bills also swiped 8 passes for 263 yards. He returned one interception 82 yards for a touchdown and finished the season with two TD interceptions.

Special Teams

Years ago, special teams players (kicking, punting) were considered the weakest on the team. If players couldn't make the starting lineup, they ended up on special teams.

That's no longer true. Today, place kickers, punters, and their supporting cast are vital to a team's success. If a team doesn't have someone who can kick the ball through the uprights in overtime or punt the ball 50 yards when the team is backed up in its own end zone, it can't be a championship team. (Kickers are often the leading point scorers in the NFL.) And if a team allows its opponent to consistently return kickoffs and punts 20 or more yards, it can't win.

Kick and punt returners can drastically change the momentum of a game—and sometimes break it wide open. There is nothing more spectacular than a zig-zagging 60-, 80-, or 100-yard return for a touchdown.

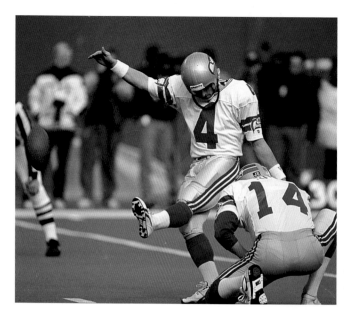

Special team players are an important part of all winning teams.

Punters

In 1992, no one punted the ball better than Greg Montgomery of the AFC's Houston Oilers. Montgomery booted the ball 53 times for a 46.9 yard average. His longest punt traveled 66 yards.

In the NFC, Harry Newsome of the Minnesota Vikings booted the ball 72 times for a 45.0 average. One punt traveled 84 yards!

Greg Montgomery was the NFL's best punter in 1992.

NFL Leading Punters

Player	No.	Yds.	Long	Avg.
Greg Montgomery, Houston Oilers	53	2,487	66	46.9
Harry Newsome, Minnesota Vikings	72	3,243	84	45.0

NFL Leading Kickers

Player	Pat	FG	Long	Pts.
Pete Stoyanovich, Miami Dolphins	34-36	30-37	53	124
Morten Andersen, New Orleans Saints	33-34	29-34	52	120
Chip Lohmiller, Washington Redskins	30-30	30-40	53	120

Kickers

In 1992, kicker Pete Stoyanovich of the AFC's Miami Dolphins led the NFL in scoring with 124 points. He made 34 of 36 extra point attempts and booted 30 of 37 field goals.

Morten Andersen of the New Orleans Saints and Chip Lohmiller of the Washington Redskins tied for first as the top placekickers in the NFC. Anderson missed only one extra point all year (33-for-34) and converted 29 of 34 field goal attempts for 120 points. Lohmiller made all 30 of his extra point attempts, and converted 30 of 40 field goal tries for 120 points.

Pete Stoyanovich led all NFL kickers with 124 points.

Punt Returns

In 1992, Johnny Bailey of the Phoenix Cardinals led the NFC and the NFL in punt returns. The shifty, fleet-footed Bailey scampered an average of 13.2 yards with the 20 punts he received. Though Bailey did not score any touchdowns, his longest return was 65 yards. Kelvin Martin of the Dallas Cowboys finished second in the NFL with 42 punt returns and a 12.7 yard average. He returned two punts for touchdowns—including a 79-yard scamper.

In the AFC, Rod Woodson of the Pittsburgh Steelers finished with 32 punt returns and an 11.4 yard average. His longest—an 80-yarder—was returned for a touchdown. Clarence Verdin of the Indianapolis Colts finished with an 11.2 yard average on 24 punts. He returned two punts for touchdowns—including an 84-yard run.

Johnny Bailey had the best average of all the NFL punt returners.

NFL Punt Return Leaders

Player	No.	Yds.	Avg.	Long	TD.
Johnny Bailey, Phoenix Cardinals	20	263	13.2	65	0
Kelvin Martin, Dallas Cowboys	42	532	12.7	79	2
Vai Sikahema, Philadelphia Eagles	40	503	12.6	87	1
Rod Woodson, Pittsburgh Steelers	32	364	11.4	80	1
Clarence Verdin, Indianapolis Colts	24	268	11.2	84	2

Joh Vaughn led the NFL in kick returns in 1992.

NFL Kick Return Leaders					
Player	**No.**	**Yds.**	**Avg.**	**Long**	**TD.**
Jon Vaughn, New England Patriots	20	564	28.2	100	1
Deion Sanders, Atlanta Falcons	40	1,067	26.7	99	2

Kick Returns

The NFL's leading kick returner in 1992 was the AFC's Jon Vaughn of the New England Patriots. The speedy Vaughn grabbed 20 kickoffs and returned them for a total of 564 yards and an amazing 28.2 yard average. Vaughn returned only one kick-off for a touchdown, but it was an NFL-best 100-yarder!

In the NFC, the Atlanta Falcons' Deion Sanders was the shiftiest kick-off returner. "Neon" Deion snatched 40 kick-offs for 1,067 total yards and a 26.7 average. Sanders returned 2 of those kicks for touchdowns—including a 99-yarder.

NFL Coach of the Year

The coach of an NFL football team has a thankless job. If a team wins, the players get all the credit. If the team loses, it's all the coach's fault. And he will probably lose his job.

Coaching million-dollar players is no easy task either. A coach has to keep egos in line while trying to get everyone to play as a team. Then there are all the hidden strategies, offensive and defensive alignments, and play-calling that a coach makes during each game.

Don Shula won back-to-back Coach of the Year awards in 1970 & 1971

Today, coaches need computer skills to keep up with all the information they need to successfully manage a team. Coaching is a year-round job. It involves many hours of studying opponents on film and analyzing the college draft. Coaches hold midnight meetings with assistant coaches, players—and sometimes meddling club owners. In addition to all of this, the media and fans keep a close eye on the team.

Fortunately for coaches, there is an award for outstanding performance. The AP polls a nationwide media panel. *The Sporting News* bases its selection on the votes of NFL coaches.

Coaches don't have to win the Super Bowl to capture the award. But they do have to win. Multiple coach of the year winners include Bill Walsh (1981, 1984) Mike Ditka (1985, 1988), and Don Shula (1970, 1971).

1992 NFL Coach of the Year	
Coach	**AP Votes**
Bill Cowher, Pettsburgh Steelers	23
Bobby Ross, San Diego Chargers	20
Mike Holmgren, Green Bay Packers	9.5
Dennis Green, Minnesota Vikings	8
George Seifert, San Francisco 49ers	7
Ted Marchibroda, Indianapolis Colts	6
Jimmy Johnson, Dallas Cowboys	5
Jim Mora, New Orleans Saints	0.5

The 1992 NFL Coach of the Year

According to AP and *The Sporting News,* the 1992 NFL Coach of the Year award went to Bill Cowher of the Pittsburgh Steelers. Cowher beat a strong field of other rookie coaches to win the award.

At 35 years old, Cowher is the second-youngest coach in the NFL. He received 23 of 79 votes from a nationwide panel of media members. Cowher edged out Bobby Ross of the San Diego Chargers.

Cowher guided the Steelers from a 7-9 record in 1991 to 11-5 and the AFC title. It was Pittsburgh's first division crown since 1984 and its best record since winning its last Super Bowl after the 1979 season. Cowher is the first Pittsburgh coach to win the award since it first was given in 1957. He replaced Chuck Noll, the most successful coach in the team's history.

"When you have team success," Cowher said, "the personal accolades will come. You can't have success merely as individuals. You've got to do it as a team."

Bill Cowher of the Pittsburgh Steelers was the 1992 NFL Coach of the Year.

Pro Bowl Team

Being named to the Pro Bowl (played in Honolulu, Hawaii, since 1980) is the crowning achievement for the best players of the year. League players and coaches select players from each position (offense and defense). Because the votes of their peers determine who will make the team, the honor is even more rewarding.

The Pro Bowl began in 1939 as a postseason All-Star game between the new league champion and a team of professional all-stars. Since 1971, the contest has featured the NFC vs. the AFC.

Tight End Jay Novacek

1992 Pro Bowl Players–NFC

Offense

Wide Receivers
*Jerry Rice, San Francisco 49ers
*Sterling Sharpe, Green Bay Packers
 Michael Irvin, Dallas Cowboys
 Andre Rison, Atlanta Falcons

Tackles
*Gary Zimmerman, Minnesota Vikings
*Lomas Brown, Detroit Lions
 Steve Wallace, San Francisco 49ers

Guards
*Randall McDaniel, Minnesota Vikings
*Guy McIntyre, San Francisco 49ers
 Nate Newton, Dallas Cowboys

Centers
*Joel Hilgenberg, New Orleans Saints
 Mark Stepnoski, Dallas Cowboys

Tight Ends
*Jay Novacek, Dallas Cowboys
 Brent Jones, San Francisco 49ers

*Starter

Quarterbacks
*Steve Young, San Francisco 49ers
 Troy Aikman, Dallas Cowboys
 Brett Farve, Green Bay Packers

Running Backs
*Emmitt Smith, Dallas Cowboys
*Barry Sanders, Detroit Lions
 Ricky Watters, San Francisco 49ers
 Rodney Hampton, New York Giants

Defense

Ends
*Reggie White, Philadelphia Eagles
*Chris Doleman, Minnesota Vikings
 Clyde Simmons, Philadelphia Eagles

Interior Linemen
*Pierce Holt, San Francisco 49ers
 Henry Thomas, Minnesota Vikings

Outside Linebackers
*Pat Swilling, New Orleans Saints
*Rickey Jackson, New Orleans Saints
 Wilber Marshall, Washington Redskins

Inside Linebackers
*Sam Mills, New Orleans Saints
*Jessie Tuggle, Atlanta Braves
 Vaughan Johnson, New Orleans Saints

Cornerbacks
*Deion Sanders, Atlanta Falcons
*Audray McMillian, Minnesota Vikings
 Eric Allen, Philadelphia Eagles

Safeties
*Tim McDonald, Phoenix Cardinals
*Chuck Cecil, Green Bay Packers
 Todd Scott, Minnesota Vikings

Specialists
 Punter–Rich Camarillo, Phoenix Cardinals
 Kicker–Morten Andersen, New Orleans Saints
 Kick Return Specialist–Mel Gray, Detroit Lions
 Special Teamer–Elbert Shelley, Atlanta Falcons

*Defensive End
Reggie White*

Cornerback Deion Sanders

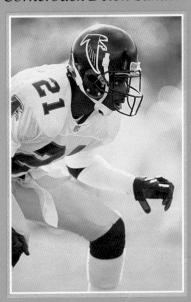

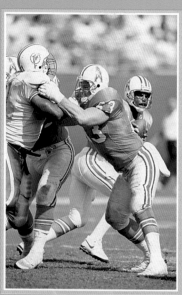

Wide Receiver
Anthony Miller

Guard Mike Munchak

1992 Pro Bowl Players–AFC

Offense

Wide Receivers
*Anthony Miller, San Diego Chargers
*Haywood Jeffires, Houston Oilers
 Andre Reed, Buffalo Bills
 Curtis Duncan, Houston Oilers
 Earnest Givins, Houston Oilers

Tackles
*Richmond Webb, Miami Dolphins
*Howard Ballard, Buffalo Bills
 Will Wolford, Buffalo Bills

Guards
*Mike Munchak, Houston Oilers
*Steve Wisniewski, L.A. Raiders
 Carlton Haselrig, Pittsburgh Steelers

Centers
*Bruce Matthews, Houston Oilers
 Dermontti Dawson, Pittsburgh Steelers

Tight Ends
*Keith Jackson, Miami Dolphins
 Marv Cook, New England Patriots

Quarterbacks
*Dan Marino, Miami Dolphins
 Warren Moon, Houston Oilers
 Jim Kelly, Buffalo Bills

Running Backs
*Barry Foster, Pittsburgh Steelers
*Thurman Thomas, Buffalo Bills
 Lorenzo White, Houston Oilers
 Harold Green, Cincinnati Bengals

Defense

Ends
*Bruce Smith, Buffalo Bills
*Leslie O'Neal, San Diego Chargers
 Neil Smith, Kansas City Chiefs

Interior Linemen
*Cortez Kennedy, Seattle Seahawks
 Ray Childress, Houston Oilers

Outside Linebackers
*Derrick Thomas, Kansas City Chiefs
*Bryan Cox, Miami Dolphins
 Cornelius Bennett, Buffalo Bills

Inside Linebackers
*Junior Seau, San Diego Chargers
*Al Smith, Houston Oilers
 Michael Brooks, Denver Broncos

Cornerbacks
*Rod Woodson, Pittsburgh Steelers
*Gill Byrd, San Diego Chargers
 Terry McDaniel, L.A. Raiders

Safeties
*Henry Jones, Buffalo Bills
*Steve Atwater, Denver Broncos
 Eugene Robinson, Seattle Seahawks

Specialists
 Punter–Rohn Stark, Indianapolis Colts
 Kicker–Nick Lowery, Kansas City Chiefs
 Kick Return Specialist–Clarence Verdin,
  Indianapolis Colts
 Special Teamer–Steve Tasker, Buffalo Bills

*Starter

*Interior Lineman
Cortez Kennedy*

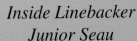

*Inside Linebacker
Junior Seau*

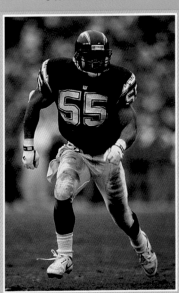

Key to Abbreviations

AFC	American Football Conference	NFL	National Football League
AP	Associated Press	NG	Noseguard
Att.	Attempts	No.	Number
Avg.	Average	NT	Nose Tackle
C	Center	OL	Offensive Lineman
CB	Cornerback	OLB	Outside Linebacker
Comp.	Completion	OT	Offensive Tackle
DB	Defensive Back	P	Punter
DE	Defensive End	Pat	Points after touchdown
DL	Defensive Lineman	Pct.	Percentage
DT	Defensive Tackle	PFWA	Pro Football Writers of America
E	End	Pos.	Position
FB	Fullback	PR	Punt Returner
FG	Field Goal	Pts.	Points
FS	Free Safety	QB	Quarterback
G	Guard	R	Rookie
GP	Games Played	RB	Running Back
GS	Games Started	RCB	Right Cornerback
HB	Halfback	RE	Right End
ILB	Inside Linebacker	Rec.	Reception
Int.	Interception	RG	Right Guard
IR	Injured Reserve	RILB	Right Inside Linebacker
K	Kicker (Placekicker)	ROLB	Right Outside Linebacker
KR	Kick Returner	RT	Right Tackle
LB	Linebacker	S	Safety
LCB	Left Cornerback	SS	Strong Safety
LE	Left End	ST	Special Teams
LG	Left Guard	T	Tackle
LILB	Left Inside Linebacker	TD	Touchdown
LOLB	Left Outside Linebacker	TE	Tight End
LT	Left Tackle	Tot.	Total
MG	Middle Guard	UPI	United Press International
Misc.	Miscellaneous	WR	Wide Receiver
MLB	Middle Linebacker	XP	Extra Points
NFC	National Football Conference	Yds.	Yards

Glossary

Blitz–A surprise defensive move in which one or more linebackers and / or safeties rush the quarterback.

Block–To check a defensive player with legal body contact.

Center–To snap the ball from the line of scrimmage.

Completion–A forward pass legally caught.

Conversion–The 1-point score made after a touchdown.

Cornerback–Either of two defensive halfbacks stationed a short distance behind the linebackers and relatively near the sidelines.

Crossbar–The horizontal bar that connects the goalpost uprights.

Defensive backfield–The four-man unit that consists of two cornerbacks and two safeties.

Defensive line–The two tackles and two ends.

Down–The period of action that starts when the ball is put in play and ends when it is dead.

End zone–The area on either end of a football field where players score touchdowns.

Extra point–The additional one-point score added after a player makes a touchdown. Teams earn extra points if the placekicker boots the ball through the uprights of the goal post, or if an offensive player crosses the goal line with the football before being tackled.

Field goal–A three-point score awarded when a placekicker boots the ball through the uprights of the goalpost.

Forward pass–A ball thrown toward the opponent's goal line.

Fumble–When a player loses control of the football.

Goal line–The line that separates the field of play from the end zone.

Goalpost–One of two upright poles at each end of the field.

Guard–An offensive or defensive lineman who plays between the tackles and center or nose guard.

Halftime–The 15-minute time period between the second and third quarters of a football game.

Handoff–When one offensive player hands the ball to another.

Hash marks–The small lines near the center of the field from which field goals are attempted.

Incompletion–A forward pass that is not caught.

Interception–When a defensive player catches a pass from an offensive player.

Kick-off–A placekick used to begin play at the start of a half or after a score.

Lineman–An offensive or defensive player positioned at the line of scrimmage.

Line of scrimmage–The imaginary line from side line to side line that divides the offense and defense.

Offense–The team that controls the ball.

Official–Any one of the seven-man officiating team that regulates play and enforces rules.

Pass–To throw the ball.

Pass interference–Illegally interfering with a player's chance to catch a forward pass or make an interception.

Penalty–A punishment given by an official to a team for a rule violation.

Placekicker–An offensive player who kicks extra points and field goals. The placekicker also kicks the ball from a tee to the opponent after his team has scored.

Pocket–The protected area formed by the five interior linemen from which the quarterback throws.

Possession–A player or team who holds and controls the ball long enough to perform any act common to the game.

Punt–To kick the ball to the opponent.

Punt return–The runback of a punt.

Quarter–One of four 15-minute time periods that makes up a football game.

Quarterback–The backfield player who usually calls the signals for the plays.

Return–A runback of a kick, punt, or an intercepted pass.

Running back–A backfield player who usually runs with the ball.

Rush–To run with the football.

Sack–To tackle the quarterback behind the line of scrimmage.

Safety–A defensive back who plays behind the linemen and linebackers. Also, two points awarded for tackling an offensive player in his own end zone when he's carrying the ball.

Side lines–The lines at each side of the field that extend from end line to end line.

Snap–To pass the football from the center to the quarterback.

Special teams–Squads of football players that perform special tasks (for example, kick-off team and punt-return team).

Tackle–An offensive or defensive lineman who plays between the ends and the guards.

Tight end–An offensive lineman who is stationed next to the tackles, and who usually blocks or catches passes.

Touchback–When the ball is dead on or behind a team's own goal line.

Touchdown–When one team crosses the goal line of the other team's end zone. A touchdown is worth six points.

Turnover–Losing the ball by a fumble or interception.

Wide receiver–An offensive player who is stationed relatively close to the sidelines and who usually catches passes.

Yardage–Distance lost or gained by the offensive team on each play. Also distance given up by the defense.

Yard line–Any of the lines marked at 5-yard intervals across the field and between the two goal lines.